# TRAVEL TALES OF MY FATHER MR. JONES

UWEM MBOT UMANA

Copyright © 2023 Uwem Mbot Umana

All rights reserved. This book or any portion thereof may not be reproduced or used in any manner whatsoever without the express written permission of the publisher, except for the use of brief quotations in a book review or scholarly journal.

Published in the United Kingdom by Uwem Mbot Umana
www.enrichyourmind.co.uk
2023

Edited and formatted by C. M. Okonkwo
(www.cmokonkwo.com)

ISBN: 9798859670536

**TRAVEL TALES OF MY FATHER MR. JONES**

# *CONTENTS*

|   | Acknowledgements | i |
|---|---|---|
|   | Foreword | iii |
| 1 | Travel Tales of My Father Mr. Jones – Part 1 | 1 |
| 2 | Travel Tales of My Father Mr. Jones – Part 2 | 7 |
| 3 | Travel Tales of My Father Mr. Jones – Part 3 | 17 |
| 4 | Nature's fury | 23 |
| 5 | Hazza | 31 |
| 6 | Patto | 45 |
| 7 | Remember Mark | 63 |
| 8 | The Drums Called Him | 71 |
| 9 | The Fight: From the diary of Mr. Akpan, another teacher at SHC | 79 |
| 10 | The Tunnel | 89 |

*TRAVEL TALES OF MY FATHER MR. JONES*

## ACKNOWLEDGEMENTS

Special thanks go to the EYM team: Abraham Kabba, editor – C. M. Okonkwo, Aspen Media graphic designer, and Sharon, John, and Pearl Umana, who have always been my first audience.

A special thanks to Dr. Emad Ayyash (British University in Dubai) and his master's students class of Discourse Analysis for autumn term of 2022, for requesting these stories for his students and all their feedback as well.

To all my fans, thank you and keep reading EYM stories.

***TRAVEL TALES OF MY FATHER MR. JONES***

**_TRAVEL TALES OF MY FATHER MR. JONES_**

# *FOREWORD*

In the charming world of literature, short stories have earned a remarkable status because of their matchless ability to move our emotions and engage our thoughts, in style, in brevity, and in profoundness. The pages of this collection will inspire your hearts and minds to begin a journey of reflection, empathy, and insights that are fuelled by interactions with the characters and the events that touch our lives in many respects.

What distinguishes Mr Uwem's writing style is its ability to move back and forth between the familiar and the extraordinary. You see the characters of his stories everywhere around you, you live the events of his stories on regular basis in your daily life, but what

## *TRAVEL TALES OF MY FATHER MR. JONES*

is extremely exceptional is that the interactions between the characters and the events will leave an unforgettable impact on your soul.

This collection of short stories possesses the power of making every day human experience a moment of reflection. The events are commonplace, yet revealing and thought-provoking. In these pages, you will delve into worlds of love and loss, hope and despair, happiness and tragedy. The momentum of feelings shining from these stories will resonate within you long after you've read the last line and turned the final page.

The author of this collection weaves his unique perspective, social background, and storytelling style into a rich textile of stories that mirror the bigger intricate web of our world. This trove of stories celebrates the art of storytelling in all that it means.

These stories will invite you to step into the shoes of characters who may be considerably different from you, yet whose fights, defeats and triumphs will strike a chord within your own heart and mind. In this collection, you will encounter the beauty and complexity of the human experience in all its diverse shades.

I've known the author of this collection for years before life decided to split us and place us in two distant countries. However, knowing the unique quality of the short stories written by my old friend, I encouraged my post-graduate students in a discourse analysis course to touch base with Mr Uwem and analyse some of the stories he wrote for this collection. I told them, "Prepare yourselves for an unforgettable experience." And so it was. As they embarked on this voyage through the pages, they immersed themselves in each story and expressed their admiration of the stories and their writing style. I am confident that you will experience the same, dear reader.

Within this collection lies the magic of storytelling—the power to illuminate, to inspire us all. Just open your heart and mind, dear reader, and allow these narratives to interact with your inner self. Enjoy, reflect, and learn.

Dr. Emad A. S. Abu-Ayyash<br>
Associate professor – TESOL.

## *TRAVEL TALES OF MY FATHER MR. JONES*

# 1: TRAVEL TALES OF MY FATHER MR. JONES – PART 1

I was on holiday with my daddy to Nigeria. My father, Mr. Jones is from the southeastern part of Nigeria. His Nigerian name is Ikpeadiamkpo. My father, as the story goes, left Nigeria in the late eighties for the US to seek greener pastures. When he got to the United States, a lot of folks could not pronounce his name, so he adopted a new name, 'Mr. Jones'. His main reason for adopting the name was that he wanted his name to sound like the Americans.

My dad had a supposedly good friend then called Mr. Wymne, who had told my father that anytime he wanted to visit the States, he could come to stay with him. On this note of invitation, my father decided to

## TRAVEL TALES OF MY FATHER MR. JONES–PART 1

make New York his port of entry into America, where he hoped to reside and start a new life.

When my father arrived at LaGuardia Airport, New York, his first shock was that Mr. Wymne was not there to receive him as was previously arranged. He could deal with that because anything could have happened to prevent him from coming to receive him. He then decided to call Mr. Wymne but never got through to him. He then made it through the wintry afternoon to Staten Island, the address he had been posting letters to Mr. Wymne. On arrival at Mr. Wymne's residence, nobody was home. He rang the doorbell over and over again. He saw a Cherokee Jeep parked in the driveway. He was confused and didn't know what to do. To make matters worse, what dad wore as a winter jacket could at best cope well with spring. By this time, dad was literally freezing. His teeth were chattering, and if you tapped his ears, he would receive no signal. It then dawned on him that once again, life had thrown a twist at him.

Mr. Wymne's neighbour, Mrs. Winterhill took pity on my dad. She had been watching from her window at the stranger who looked weather-beaten and would not go away. My dad never understood the meaning of winter. If he had, he would not have done such a disservice to himself by dressing that way in New York in the middle of winter. My dad was freezing to death. When my dad rang the doorbell of the Winterhills, Mrs. Clara Winterhill did not hesitate to open the door.

The first words that escaped from my dad's lips were, "Can I please sit next to the fire? I am dying of cold."

The lady positioned my father next to the radiator and made him a hot cup of tea with a toast.

My dad had a glimpse of what heaven would be like after he was taken in by Mrs. Winterhill.

"Oh I miss Lagos, how I miss Lagos" my dad chimed.

A little toddler kept rattling, "Who is he, mammy? He looks very lost."

Clara replied, "He is a traveller who has just arrived from across the Atlantic."

"What is 'Atlantic', mammy?" the toddler carried on.

## TRAVEL TALES OF MY FATHER MR. JONES–PART 1

"A big sea of water that is so big that you can find whales in them."

My dad explained to Clara what had just befallen him and showed his passport to prove to Clara that he had just arrived from Nigeria. Not having anywhere to go from the airport, he had to find his way to Wymne's house. Mrs. Winterhill offered that he must have been stuck or something as she was sure she had seen him that morning. Daddy and Mrs. Winterhill conversed until night crept upon them.

The snow had been unusually heavy that day, so Mrs. Winterhill could not send daddy away. She had to call her husband at work to explain the confused situation she found herself in. Should she send a stranger out into the biting cold or stay with an unknown man in a house without her husband because she wanted to be a good woman?

My daddy said that he overheard the woman say to the person on the other end of the phone, "I can't. You needed to see how he was shivering when he came in. He is fresh from Africa, where it is nice and sunny compared to this miserable frosty season."

The woman must have accidentally pressed the speaker button on the phone when dad overheard the person on the other end of the call say, "I don't want him in my house. Before I get back, I want him outta my house."

Too late, dad had heard it!

When the woman came out from the adjoining room where she had had the telephone conversation, dad was already gathering his stuff and saying, "It's getting late. I must leave. Thanks for everything, Mrs. Winterhill."

The lady asked dad, "Leave, to where?" and dad said he didn't know. The lady knew she could not take the risk of being alone with this total stranger, yet something on the inside of her felt so sorry for my dad.

"I will at least fix you some hot dinner before you leave," Clara said.

My dad ate the dinner and did not have a clue what the night held in store for him. With only one hundred and fifty-two dollars in his pocket, he knew that, at least, he had tried his best in life. For a moment, he fast-forwarded his life ten years and the

## *TRAVEL TALES OF MY FATHER MR. JONES–PART 1*

picture he saw was bright and beautiful. He saw himself in a nice cozy home with warmth and lots of space around. He saw his wife and children in the living room playing the piano and violin while he sang, "Our God, is an awesome God, He reigns…" The door unlocked at that moment, and a man walked into the room truncating dad's daydreaming.

My dad narrowed his eyes as if he had seen an apparition, but it wasn't an apparition; it was real.

"Sam?" my father called out.

"Epe?" the man, Samuel called back, totally lost. That was the name my dad was called in Monrovia because they could not pronounce his name 'Ikpeadiamkpo'.

## 2: TRAVEL TALES OF MY FATHER MR. JONES – PART 2

My daddy had travelled to Liberia in the late seventies for a conference at the University of Liberia, Monrovia. He remembers the workshop session on 'The development of Democracy in the West African sub region' that was facilitated by a man from Fourah Bah College, Sierra Leone, a certain Mr. Samuel Winterhill. Samuel Winterhill had been in Sierra Leone for only two months and thought he knew enough to see himself as an expert in West African politics. The fact that he was a black American who researched the political development, or rather, underdevelopment of West Africa, did not

## TRAVEL TALES OF MY FATHER MR. JONES–PART 2

mean he was the best expert that everybody should listen to. He had a certain intellectual arrogance about him. He thought that because he had come from the United States, everybody should listen to him, and dad clearly challenged him on a number of his submissions. To begin with, dad argued that the sub-region was too big a demography for him to study. It had to be narrowed down. Samuel claimed that he had the intellectual capacity and capability to deal with that range of demography, which was quite undermining to the other scholars present. They had this robust debate, which almost marred the success of the workshop. They, afterwards, met at the university's staff club that night and shared a few rounds of beverages and local delicacies. Ten years later, these two men stood facing each other in the most unimaginable circumstance.

For two days, Wymne did not return, and his cell phone was switched off. The next place where my dad knew somebody was Ohio. He made contact with Tari in Ohio. Tari asked him to come over straightaway.

## *TRAVEL TALES OF MY FATHER MR. JONES*

Sometimes in life, you just come across people who do not struggle to be of assistance to others, and sometimes, you come across folks who make you understand that they do not owe you any obligation. "This is what makes life beautiful and diverse," my dad always said.

My dad thanked the Winterhills for their hospitality and left for Ohio to meet Tari, who was kind enough to put him up for a couple of weeks. With almost zero finance and long distances to cover, my dad began his American adventure.

Every time my dad narrated his American expedition story to me, it always came with a new kind of gusto. He told me the story over twenty times, and I looked forward to each session because each session revealed something fresh.

For documentation purposes, Tari advised my dad to go to the state of Texas, because it was supposedly easier to get a driver's license there so that he would have a form of identification. On the good old Greyhound did my father hop on, destination – Austin, Texas.

## *TRAVEL TALES OF MY FATHER MR. JONES–PART 2*

My father has never travelled on such a long stretch before in his entire life. This was a journey of 1,900km. New York to Cleveland was only 755km. My dad thought that was bad, but imagine this phase of his adventure with zero finance.

Within two months of arrival in Texas, my dad got a driver's license. I can still see the way his face lit up, when he said, "For once in over three months of a hard life, I had something to celebrate, some sort of accomplishment." This encouraged him so much. While at Austin, his eyes caught the attention of the phrase 'north to the future'. That was how he got the epiphany of 'fast forward'. Whenever he was going through rough times, he would always fast forward a few months and years ahead, to that life he had always wanted to live. The challenges of the moment would count as nothing compared to his destination in life.

For my dad, right from the first day he landed his feet on American soil, life was full of twists and turns. He kept holding on to the image of the kind of life he imagined himself living in America. That dream never left him. So, what about 'north to the future?' Since his life was in such a state of a labyrinth and almost rudderless, he needed something to serve as an anchor point for him, and that was the official state motto for Alaska. He had never heard of Alaska before then. He went on to the local library to do some research about the state of Alaska. It was not like now when you could ask Google anything from your palm-held device and get an instant result. Back in the early eighties, you had to visit the library or resource centre to look for answers.

My dad was fascinated by what he found out about the state of Alaska. He loved the fact that Alaska was not a popular state, not top on the list for holidaymakers, not top of the list for retirees, not top of the list for job seekers, not top of the list for students, and the list was endless. Yet Alaska had the largest oil and gas fields in North America. Alaska had the lowest population density. It was the biggest state in the United States. It could accommodate the state of Rhode Island 425 times and was twice as big as Texas. He loved the fact that in Alaska, you would be submerged and fused with nature. Alaska was part of the Arctic Circle.

## *TRAVEL TALES OF MY FATHER MR. JONES–PART 2*

He struck something profound during his research. Alaska had the highest record temperature in 1915, which was a hundred degrees Fahrenheit, and the lowest record temperature was in 1971, which was a minus eighty degrees Fahrenheit. He fell in love with Alaska. No wonder he named me 'Denali', after the highest mountain peak in Alaska, my brother 'Yukon', after the Yukon River in Alaska, and my sister 'Ptarmigan', after the state bird Willow Ptarmigan. That was how my dad ended up in Alaska.

Going to Nigeria was now becoming a regular feature of our family. My dad had a nice country home, and it was fenced around. He had built what they call in Nigeria a 'boys quarters' (BQ) at the back of the house. We had sufficient space to lounge around and relax. With the weather in Nigeria being good all year round, we could do barbecues and outdoor cooking all year round too. One thing I never understood was why that section of the house was called 'boys quarters'. Why not 'girls' quarters' or 'men's quarters', or even 'ladies' quarters'. It was all etched in the colonial mentality.

## *TRAVEL TALES OF MY FATHER MR. JONES*

When the British ruled Nigeria, they had separate quarters for the servants who served them, and since these servants were 'live-ins', they had these quarters for them. The servants were drivers, cooks, maids, and so forth. This concept came to stay in Nigeria, and, over the years, it has undergone some transformation.

In our BQ lived Old Major, who was the caretaker of the country home. Old Major was always talking about his escapades in Monrovia and Freetown during the conflict. He served in ECOMOG and was posted to Liberia and Sierra Leone. When he came back from the posting, he was discharged and on reserve. He had an old rifle that he kept as a souvenir for himself. He spent his Saturday mornings oiling the rifle. He kept the country home clean and gave a sense of security to the property. He mowed the lawns and trimmed the trees and flowers. He watered the plants and kept the outside perimeter of the gates and fence clean. He took care of the dogs and took them for walks and exercise. He loved his job. He did not have a wife or kids. Rumours had it that he got

## *TRAVEL TALES OF MY FATHER MR. JONES–PART 2*

shot in his genitals during the conflict and could not reproduce, so he chose to now live as a hermit.

He was well-known in the village and was dreaded. He also made a lot of money from people who wanted to see my dad. He told them they had to book an appointment to see 'Oga', a local term for boss. He had a friend who was a palm wine tapper. This friend of his, Obulu, supplied him with free wine because anytime my dad was around, Obulu supplied my dad with fresh palm wine at triple the normal cost. His wine, according to Old Major was not diluted and was the best in the entire community. That was why his wine was booked weeks in advance. However, because of the special relationship and respect that Obulu had for Old Major, anytime my dad was around, he halted his supplies to other customers and delivered only to my dad. My dad needed this wine to entertain the stream of visitors who were always visiting him.

I found it quite surprising that lots of people always came to visit my dad anytime we were around. From the minute we woke up till when we retired to bed, folks were always coming to see him. I once asked him, "Why do so many people come to see you? Where were these people when life was dealing a hard blow on you in America?" My dad would reply, "What have they to do with it? Did they send me to America? They don't owe me anything."

I never understood, but as I got older, I began to appreciate why. When the economic realities of the community opened up to me, I knew that my dad was doing the right thing.

*TRAVEL TALES OF MY FATHER MR. JONES–PART 2*

## 3: TRAVEL TALES OF MY FATHER MR. JONES – PART 3

"*I used to trek everywhere. In the village, I trekked to the farm, trekked to the stream, trekked to the market, trekked to the village square, trekked to the local school, and also trekked to visit family. The only thing I had was my 'legedes benz'. I loved it. I cherished it. It meant so much to me.*" ~ Ikpeadiamkpo, a.k.a. Mr. Jones.

One of the things that I enjoyed doing with my dad was going for walks. We always walked in Fairbanks, and even when we moved to Anchorage, we didn't stop doing that as well. Anytime dad was away, Yukon, Ptarmigan, Mum, and I would go for walks with the dogs. We used to call it the 'family

## *TRAVEL TALES OF MY FATHER MR. JONES–PART 3*

walk'. It was a culture that dad brought to America with him. He said that when he was in Nigeria, he walked a lot, and it formed part and parcel of him. He used the term 'trek', which sent me to the dictionary. Not because he enjoyed walking but because he had no other option than to walk. When he arrived in America, he did not have money to eat healthy food. He was eating tons of junk food.

So, the only service he could do for himself was walk away the pounds and stay fit as well. He walked everywhere walkable. On average, he was walking about twenty-five kilometres a day. He didn't have money for a gym membership and also couldn't afford a car in his early years, so he took public transport where applicable and walked the rest of the way.

When he was stabilised, he carried on with this good old habit, and I can still hear him loud and clear saying to us, "Keep your life simple. Devise a lifestyle that will work for you. With walking, and running, you only need a pair of trainers and you are good. No one will ask you to pay for walking on the street." We would all laugh.

## *TRAVEL TALES OF MY FATHER MR. JONES*

In Ntanda village in Nigeria, my dad would take me and Yukon for walks. We would go to see plots of land that he owned, his animals, and his plantations. We would visit relatives and the local schools. We would go to local churches and participate in village events. My dad made sure we attended initiation celebrations, launching parties, funerals, marriages, and 'mismarriage' ceremonies. We made local friends and interacted with them.

These local friends would come to visit us and want to stay overnight, and I would always ask them to go back to their homes. Why? Because my dad always said to me, "Learn to be content with what you have, and enjoy what you have till the next one comes along." Yes, we might have been more privileged than most of them but we had also experienced rough times, times of lack and of uncertainties.

These walks opened my eyes to the harsh economic realities of the moment. We had choices – choice of food, schools, clothing, language, and dreams, and there were people who did not have a choice.

## *TRAVEL TALES OF MY FATHER MR. JONES–PART 3*

Life presented one side to them, and they believed in that one side and lived that one side. Life presented a particular music to them and they only danced to that tune of music. The very thing that made my daddy leave Nigeria was replaying right in front of me. He had tried hard to change the tune, he had tried hard to change the perspective, he had tried hard to dream a dream and live it, but it did not work for him, so, he left. I could see that history before my very eyes. I could see his people, my people, resigned to fate. I could see the people helpless and crying out for help. I could see the people staring at us and wondering whether we lived on the same planet. They wondered why we were so different from them. If only they knew that my dad made a choice, a choice to change his destiny.

These were my people. These were my kinsmen. They have all been sold out by their leaders, they have all been bought over by the richer politicians, and they have all been numbed by poverty. They have lost loved ones because there was no money to pay for hospital bills, and they have lost family lands because they have to raise money to bury a family member. How about selling that same land to pay school fees? Doesn't that baffle your imagination? They would rather sell a plot of land to bury someone, a dead person than sell that same land to train someone in the university.

My people were living a lie. They had been deceived. That was why my dad took us on these village walks. I fast-forwarded. A year from now, how and where do I see my kinsmen? When we were planning for our yearly pilgrimage to the village for the following year, we had shipped a container ahead of us. In this container were old clothes, used books, used computers for the village school, old iPads, printers, and items that would help empower the people.

We had printed the programme for the summer – leadership training for the local youth free of charge, language lessons, applied math course, life skills, thinking skills courses. I fast forwarded again, and Yukon said he could see the people create a life for themselves, believe in themselves, and live their lives. Even Ptarmigan and my mum would act as facilitators in the summer programme. History would be made in Ntanda village.

My people have a right to dream. They have a right to fastforward their lives to see that the picture it holds is bright.

## 4: NATURE'S FURY

Juan was screaming and yelling. The fire chief tried to console her.

"Send helicopters in there! Send helicopters in there! My whole family is trapped in there," she yelled.

The fire chief ushered her to safety. She needed to be evacuated. Mothers were crying, children were crying, and men were out there trying to see if there was an iota of hope left. The air was stricken with grief and torment, and it was like hell. The earth was angry. The earth had unleashed her fury on the residents of this little village of Escuintla.

## *NATURE'S FURY*

There was no serious prior indication. The geologists picked up the waves and signal a little late and by the time warning was issued, disaster had already struck. There was no time to pack out of the community. That is the thing about nature, it can be so unpredictable and can deal such a foul blow sometimes.

The Volcano of Fire – VoF hadn't erupted in tens of years. It seemed like all this while, she was brewing the molten lava. Suddenly it burst forth. The earth could not contain her anymore, and the hot liquid found its way to the surface of the earth, travelling up to forty miles away and about 5,000 metres above sea level. The villages worst hit were Los Lotes and El Rodeo. People were melted alive, being covered in hot fluid while they still drew breath. What a drastic way to die. People scampered for safety. Emergency services arrived. Not very much could be done because of poor visibility and the volcanic ash in the air. Planes could not land, and copters could not fly. It was bad. Really bad.

There was a need to get the few people out of the village. Juan wouldn't want to go. Her three children were in the inferno. Her husband was inside that hot liquid. Her mother and father were missing and her relatives had all disappeared. At a moment of the earth unleashing her fury, there had been a huge divide between her life filled with people, sadness, emotion-laden, sorrow, grief, uncertainty, fear, and loneliness. This was what nature unleashing its terror did to the quiet village of Escuintla in Guatemala.

Juan had spent her whole life dreaming of when she would eventually be free and such a proud mother. Years of toiling and nursing her family seemed to dissolve right before her eyes. The nights she spent at the hospital with her daughter Maria, when she had to go through a medical procedure to correct the deformity in her bones. The times she spent in the United States for further surgeries and how she nurtured her daughter back to life again. She started school hobbling, being the centre of teasing, and finally after all the surgeries, she began to stabilise, began to walk, then run, and ended up sprinting for her school. Thereafter she graduated from primary school to high school with flying colours. Maria proceeded to high school and became a flyer, in both academics and sporting events. She was the cynosure of all eyes. Juan's husband Esplendido worked in the sugar fields from morning till night, six days a week to provide succour for the family.

Maria graduated amongst the best top ten in her high school and left for the States to study medicine. She was on a scholarship. She was like the light of the family. Considering how she was born deformed and all the medical journey the family had to go through to get her to walk, it was a miracle that she did not only excel in academics but also in sports.

It was normal for her to visit her parents and siblings during her holidays. She loved spending time with her mum and siblings. Her physical presence always generated a lot of warmth and hope, not just for her immediate family but for those from the community. Her story was alive. Her presence generated hope for hopeless people because of her turnaround in life. And then the cruel hands of disaster snatched her away. Juan could not take it. Where was Esplendido? He was missing. Juan's aged parents could not make it out. They were frail, and that's why they had moved in to stay with the Esplendidos so that they could be supported. When the few people saw the inferno rolling over, the hot liquid cascading down, they took off. Again, nature played a trick on the physically challenged and it was so difficult to leave loved ones behind. It was either you scampered for safety or you stayed back and got roasted with them.

In the pandemonium that broke out, people ran helter-skelter. No one really took notice of who was with who. The keywords were 'survival', 'flee', and 'safety'. It was until one reached a relatively safe place that family members were sought for and headcount was taken. That was when the reality dawned on folks that the much-dreaded thought of 'Were they trapped?' started playing on people's minds.

You would not want to, in the slightest imagination, think that your family had been melted by the dreary liquid or suffocated in the heat that accompanied the liquid. That death was too severe and harsh to contemplate, yet in the starkest reality, it was probably the scenario. Charred bodies and unidentifiable bodies. Of what use will DNA testing

## NATURE'S FURY

do? Give the charred body a funeral? Be settled that there is no hope or possibility that he or she could have been alive? Dread! Dread! Dread!

Babies crying, the stench of grief in the air, the emergency services overwhelmed with balancing professional work and emotionally stabilising those who made it out. It was tough! This has been the most violent eruption in more than a century. It waited till Maria had entered her final year in medical school. It waited till it was the season for Maria to come visit before it unleashed its fury. What cruelty! Juan did not lose hope. The very hopeless situation in Maria's life that was transformed into a life of expectations made Juan hopeful. It reminded Juan of Maria's favourite book – *Great Expectations* by Charles Dickens. Maria survived a hopeless childhood and turned out to be amongst the best. Juan held hope, encouraging herself that Maria somehow will be safe and those around her will be safe too. She represented that hope. She was that symbol of transcending the barriers of hopelessness. Maria is fine, she has been a survivor. She will survive this. I will see her again and all those with her will make it.

## *TRAVEL TALES OF MY FATHER MR. JONES*

Juan consoled herself as she got nudged into the truck.

*NATURE'S FURY*

# 5: HAZZA

It was a little past 11 am and I heard a rap on my classroom door.

"Come on in," I hollered.

We were on a five minutes recess and a fine tall gentleman walked in, looking calm and sober. I stood up from my chair and walked over to him. I stretched forth my hand and he received mine in a handshake. His face lit up in a smile and he embraced me. His beard was glistening and was a little longer than it used to be when he was my student a few terms back. His palm was sweaty and his brow was a little furrowed, and my mind raced back to one of my most dramatic encounters with this gentleman two years ago.

## *HAZZA*

"Hazza, can you sit down please?"

"No, Teacher."

"Hazza, can you get on with your work?"

"No, Teacher. Don't know what to do."

"Did you ask for any help?"

"No, Teacher."

"When I was explaining to the class what they had to do, you were talking and now you are stuck."

"Teacher, me don't understand English."

"Okay, I am going to help you. I am going to explain to you what you have to do. Just listen."

"Ok, Teacher."

As I leaned over to Hazza to explain what he had to do, he got engrossed with Ali on a different tangent. Ali was sitting two rows behind Hazza, and Hazza's neck was turned back talking to Ali while I was there waiting to help him.

I tapped him on the shoulder. "Hazza, you need to listen to what I have to say."

He replied, "One minute, Teacher."

An argument broke forth, and a fight had been imminent.

"Stop!" I proclaimed.

## *TRAVEL TALES OF MY FATHER MR. JONES*

I got ignored and the argument got heated. It was all in Arabic. Screams of "Teacher, Teacher" echoed all around the room.

Hazza stood up and dashed towards Ali, and at the same time, Ali jumped out of his seat and ran towards him. The whole class was tensed and punches were pulled.

It was a critical moment of decision for me. I wondered if I should act as a referee or seek help, act as an intervention officer, or as a copper. I also wondered what I would do or say to myself if I was accidentally punched.

I took a decision without further delay. Seek help.

I stepped outside the class door and requested for a military instructor to come and stop the fight.

EN, the military instructor paced down very quickly. The moment he entered the room, all the students scampered to their seats.

There was something about EN that I found quite fascinating. He was a tall man with a calm carriage. He spoke sparingly and never indulged in arguments with the students. He was always on his phone and had a rare style of a beard. He walked in calculated steps. The students dreaded him.

My first encounter with him was in the summer of 2013. I had been recently transferred to the Military department, which was tagged as MD, and I was struggling to come to terms with how things worked there. They were a couple of military training instructors, who we called MTIs. They were responsible for maintaining law and discipline amongst the students. These were ex-servicemen, who had served in various capacities in the different armies in the Middle East and also in different parts of the world. These men had loud voices. They yelled, screamed, and barged the living daylights out of these students.

At the end of each hallway in the MD was a washroom. Basically, it was a toilet. Why they decided to go the American 'washroom' way remained a mystery. There were two long hallways in the MD facility and two washrooms. There was another washroom which was for the academic staff. Then after a female staff joined us, we had to forfeit the usage rights of that toilet. The male staff was asked to use the toilet at the end of Hallway One. As was customary in that part of the world, information dissemination was an area that required further development. While some people were aware of the new development, some weren't and hence mix-ups occurred. I had gone to use the toilet at the end of Hallway One when I found out that the door was locked. Usually, it was kept open.

I was literally bursting with a bloated bladder. I needed to empty it so badly. I screamed for the keys. EN was standing not up to twenty feet away from me and didn't say a word. Finally, Crazy Omar, one of the MTIs shouted, "Mr. Blue, what's the matter?"

"I need the toilet key."

"Mr. EN has the key."

EN was standing so close. I walked up to him and requested the key from him. I then went on to berate him for being so unsympathetic. He didn't say a word.

Twenty minutes later he was at my door with Crazy Omar to ask why I was angry with him. I explained that he was standing not too far away from me while I was looking for the toilet key to empty my bladder, and he did nothing but looked at me.

## *HAZZA*

"I don't have the key," he explained.

"But I got the key from you. Crazy Omar told me to get the key from you."

"That was the master key, and no one has access to that key except me because as the Dean of Discipline, I have access to everywhere."

"Oh, really? This is news to me."

"What is news?"

"That you have a master key, that you are the Dean of Discipline, and that no person has access to the master key except you."

"I only helped you, and you should be thankful to me."

Straightaway I apologised and thanked him.

Five minutes later, I was in need of Crazy Omar. His boys were at it again. In my class, some of his boys decided to do things that were not honourable. So I poked my head out and yelled at Crazy Omar to come quickly, but he was nowhere to be found. In the promotion of esprit de corps, EN came by to bail me out. I asked him to extract four boys who were such a pain in the class. You could hear a pin drop in the silence of the class as the students awaited to hear the names of the boys that would be called out. For me, if it was possible, about eighty-nine percent of the students would be out for a drill, but knowing that it was impossible to do that, I needed to target the tougher of the toughest kids. The class was a tough one. The majority of the students were from mountainous regions and they were used to harsh circumstances.

"Ali, Sultan, Ahmed, and Hazza, please follow Mr. EN. The main culprits are Ali and Hazza," I announced. I could hear a sigh of relief from the other students who were not called out.

Two minutes later, I looked out through the window and saw the four boys standing at attention in the hot sun in cardinal positions. One was facing north, another south, the third east, and the last west. The temperature was about fifty degrees Celsius and the humidity was about eighty percent. Mr. EN was under the shade with his sunshades on, watching the boys. After their shirts had been thoroughly drenched in perspiration, Mr. EN asked them to do pushups with their knuckles on the hard concrete floor.

Twenty minutes later, Hazza walked in with Ali

## *HAZZA*

drenched in perspiration and limping. They tendered a coerced apology. Their hairs were shaven with uneven patches. What EN did to them, I did not want to imagine.

Hazza was upset with me for sending him off to Mr. EN. For the next two days, he wouldn't speak to me. He wore a grumpy face all the time in the classroom and would not even say hello to me in the corridor. He started becoming a truant. I understood how he felt. However, he needed to, most importantly, understand that certain behaviours were unacceptable in certain settings and everyone would be held accountable for their actions.

I must confess that it must be pretty embarrassing to walk about with patches of hair on your head and you were not allowed to even it out. It served as a visual reminder of what the person had done. Everybody knew what the person did and the person became a reference point. I was not too sure if that punishment would solve the problem, but the key thing was that there was the concept of consequence for inappropriate behaviour and action.

"Hazza, can you stay behind, please?"

## *TRAVEL TALES OF MY FATHER MR. JONES*

"For, what Teacher?"

"I need to speak to you."

"About what?"

"About you."

"What about me?"

"Well, I noticed that after the incident with Mr. EN you have been going about with a long face."

"Okay."

"So, I would like to know why you go about with a long face and you don't seem happy with me."

"Teacher, me happy."

"No, you're not, and you know that. You are not even looking at me in the face."

"Teacher, Ali talk bad to me and my mother, me tell Ali, stop, Ali don't stop, then me and Ali box and you call Mr. EN. This not good. Everybody hear Ali talk bad about mother."

"I may not have understood what you guys were talking about, but I asked you to stop talking, to ignore Ali, so that…"

"What this word, Teacher, 'ignore'?"

"It means 'leave that matter alone', 'forget about the issue'."

## *HAZZA*

"Ali talk bad about me mother, me forget about him, Teacher? No, Teacher, this, not good. Me tell Ali, this not good and me and Ali box."

"But I was right there to give you help because you called for help and you chose to carry on with Ali, ignoring my advice and disrupting your learning and the learning of other students."

"Sorry, Teacher."

"Listen, Hazza, I don't hate you, I like you. In fact, I love you. I want you to succeed. If you carry on like this, you are not going to succeed."

"Okay, Teacher."

"I am here to help you, and I want to help you so that you can speak good English."

"Thank you, Teacher."

I put my hand over his shoulder and walked him to the door. I saw his face beam up and a slow smile creep across his face.

From that day, things took an upward spiral for him. He started listening to me and doing his work. His motivation increased, and he was on fire. Over the next couple of months, I watched him grow from strength to strength, and everybody in the class began to make considerable progress. Our relationship grew stronger. We fought sometimes, I raised my voice sometimes, and I got frustrated most of the time, but I learnt one thing: they were never a part of what was being forced on them and this was part of the resistance.

So when he walked through the doors of classroom 16 in the Industry School to find me, I was stunned.

"How did you know I was here?"

"Teacher, I went to MD to look for you and I was told that you are in Industry School now, so I decided to come and look for you."

"Wow! That is so kind of you. Thanks for coming to say hello."

"I know you are busy, Teacher, but can I speak to you outside? Just one minute."

"Sure," I replied.

At that point, I was astounded by his courtesy, his maturity, and his sense of responsibility.

Outside the classroom, he told me how he missed me and would do anything to come and sit in my

## *HAZZA*

classroom again. He said he just wanted to come and say thank you for caring for him and his other mates. He said he never realised how great the care was until he left MD and found out that nobody loved him as I did. By that time, tears were streaming down his face.

He hugged me and wanted to take a photo with me. I was about to call on Hashim, a student of mine, to come to take a photo of us with his phone when he said, "Teacher, no need. This is selfie."

I was impressed. I felt like a celebrity when he took the selfie from different angles. At one stage, he borrowed my hat and struck a pose with it.

Finally, he requested a moment to speak with my class. Of course, I obliged him.

He spoke for about three minutes in Arabic and when he finished, I saw that some of the boys were teary. They gave him a round of applause, and I wondered what he told them in Arabic for those three minutes.

We said goodbye to each other, and I let what he said to the boys soak in as they wiped their faces.

I was still reeling in reflection on Hazza of all people coming back to Abu Dhabi to say thank you to me all the way from Ras Al Khaimah. As I was engaged with this thought, I heard the bell ring.

A smile slowly crept across my face as I watched the boys file out. I wondered how many more 'Hazzas' I had amongst those crop of boys. I silently wished that there would be one, only one, anything extra would be a bonus.

*HAZZA*

## 6: PATTO

Sitting in the derelict building with a bunch of hood boys, he drew a whiff of smoke from the rolled substance, choked and coughed. No one seemed to mind him. Everybody was in their own world, their life depended on the rolled substance. They started their day with the rolled substance, took the substance during their break time, and finished their day with it. There was something that the rolled substance gave to them; it was companionship. The rolled substance put them in a world where they belonged. They had no family or friends who cared for them, but in the little community of sharing the rolled substance, they found family, companionship, comradeship, and succour.

## *PATTO*

Patto had just returned from the big city, where he had gone to visit his paternal uncle Chief Aluede Odiase. The encounter had not been a favourable one.

"Chief, we cannot have your nephew with us. We barely know him," Augusta, Chief's wife announced.

"I understand, but he will be staying in the boy's quarters."

"Chief, he will be a bad influence on our kids."

"What influence are you talking about? Ronnie is already lost, and Edna is not doing so well."

"So must we bring in somebody that will make them even worse?"

"You do not know that, Augusta. It might be that this young boy is the spark they will need to sit up in life."

"*Mba*[1], Chief, I disagree. I do not want this boy in our house. Period!"

"Well, in that case, I will have no option than to…"

Patto interrupted, as he barged into the dining

---

[1] Igbo word, meaning 'No'.

## *TRAVEL TALES OF MY FATHER MR. JONES*

room, where his uncle, Chief, and his wife were having a conversation during breakfast.

"Good morning, Uncle. Good morning, Aunty."

"Good morning, Patto," Chief responded. "Did you sleep well?"

"Yes, sir."

"Good morning, Patto," Augusta answered.

Chief stood up, and said, "Augusta, we shall conclude the conversation when I come back from work."

"Ok, Chief."

As Chief was making his way to the car, Patto joined him.

"Uncle, I would like to go back to the village tomorrow."

"Why the rush, Patto? I have been thinking of how to support you."

"Uncle, I need to go back to help grandma in the village."

"Well, if you insist."

As Patto took a long drawn inhalation from the rolled substance, the hairs on his head stood and his head spun. That conversation kept replaying in his mind. It was clear that he was not wanted in his uncle's house. This uncle was a near relative. Since the demise of his parents, he had been to about six relatives' houses and had been rejected by all of them. He was yet to understand what crime he had committed that made everybody reject him. He still remembered the numerous relatives who visited his family home when his father was alive. Their house had been a beehive of activities. Sometimes, as one relative was leaving, another was just checking in. It was so draining. He had to constantly share his room and toys with cousins and distant relatives. He didn't have his father to himself. He was always trying to catch his father's attention. As soon as his dad returned from work, there was a stream of people waiting to see him. His dad had one weakness: he didn't know how to turn people away or ask them to come back another day. His mother would have done the job for him, but his dad would always insist that the people be allowed to have access to him, even at the expense of his quiet time and family. He would usually be through with the last guest at about 11 pm and go straight to bed because he had to wake up for work early the next morning.

Afua, Patto's dad was a chartered auditor with Royal Accounting Corporation (RAC) based in Lagos. He had travelled to Lomé, in Togo to audit a company that had a retainership with his company, as a massive fraud in the company was about to be uncovered. Afua went to sleep in his hotel room in Lomé and never woke up. A post-mortem examination revealed that he had died of poisoning. He was buried amidst pomp and pageantry from his family members. They all sang how good a man he was.

His entitlements were calculated to the tune of 23 million naira. Afua's brothers conspired with the company and took all the money. What happened to his next of kin? Did a well-schooled man like Afua not document his next of kin? Questions that required answers. They did not give Angela, Afua's wife a dime. Angela went into shock after her husband's death, then one event led to the other that culminated in her demise. She left behind three children, Patto being the eldest. The children moved

## *PATTO*

from one relative's house to another as a flock without a shepherd. Nobody wanted to take them in. It was an excuse upon excuse. The head of the family, Odiase, who collected the money from RAC would not take in Afua's children or offer any kind of support to them. Patto was too young to engage his uncle in a fight even though he knew that money was given to him. The key word for them was survival.

Patto packed his siblings, Odion and Iyase, and they went back to the village to stay with their grandmother who was advanced in age, but strong and agile. She had a medium-sized cash crop farm, which she used to support her grandchildren. Patto and his siblings all worked on the farm while they attended the village primary and secondary school. They helped their grandmother on the farm after school, and Patto did extra work on weekends to support the family. Like a few other young workers in the village, he would often go to the big market and cart goods for traders and shoppers on a rented wheelbarrow all day for a fee. He would be the only one exhausted at the end of the day and didn't understand how the others did it.

## *TRAVEL TALES OF MY FATHER MR. JONES*

"Akeem, how do you guys do this job all day and not get tired?" he asked one of the other workers.

"We take soja. Soja keeps us going."

"What's soja?"

"*Ikpo*[2]. Weed. It keeps us going."

"Aren't you too young to smoke weed? That's dangerous to your health."

"Hey, listen, I am here minding my business and you come to ask me how we get the energy to work all day. I told you, and now you want to preach me a sermon on what's good for me, eh?"

"Sorry."

"You had better be sorry for yourself."

Patto remembered his first drag of weed and how after that day he got hooked. He had found a new set of friends who had accepted him for who he was, a wheelbarrow pusher. They did not discriminate against him. He felt loved and at home after the numerous rejections he had received from his relatives. He felt wanted and grew up with these co-

---

[2] Marijuana.

smokers as his allies.

After passing his General Certificate of Education and University Matriculation Exams, he decided to try his distant wealthy uncle, whom his dad had helped at some stage in life. He was scared of being rejected again, however, his dream of attending a university pushed him to see this distant well-off uncle.

He had overheard the conversation between his uncle and his uncle's wife and knew that the problem would be with aunty, Augusta. He had offered himself that dignity to leave Chief's house before he would be ejected. He felt good about this decision, and before he left, Chief had promised to financially support him through university.

As he sat with his barrow friends and smoked, he announced to them that he would be leaving for the big city to attend university in a week.

"We know say you sabi book," Kenoski announced. "We happy well well for you, but this book thing no be for us."

"Yeah, my guy, we wish you well. Me I know say you go make am. But make you no forget us o. You

## *TRAVEL TALES OF MY FATHER MR. JONES*

know say we still dey here dey push barrow. We go dey wait you bros Patto," Ipi said.

Kenoski handed Patto five thousand naira. "Take. This na from us to support you. We no say no be big money but at least e fit help buy you smoke when you dey study."

They all cracked up.

"Patto no go need joint when him dey read those big books. Na after him don read the big books, him go need the joint to relax him mind. I don tell you say, your head na empty head, nothing dey inside this your empty head."

Patto was moved to tears, as he accepted the money. It wasn't the money that moved him to tears, but the fact that these were the only true friends he had in his life. They had accepted him and given him a sense of belonging in life. When all his extended family turned him away, these guys let him into their lives. For that, he was so grateful.

The night before his departure, his seventy-five-year-old grandma sat him and his siblings down for a meeting.

"Odion and Iyase, you know that Patto is leaving

us tomorrow for the city to start higher school. I pray that our gods will go with him and guide him through his stay there."

"*Isee*[3]," they all chorused.

"May you walk only in light."

"*Isee*," they chanted.

"May the evil eyes never see you."

"*Isee*," the chorus continued.

"And may you come out successful in your endeavours and bring back the Golden Fleece."

"*Isee* o!"

"Since *Aluede* has made this dream come true, may his path never dim."

"*Isee* o."

"May his wife Augusta, and their children prosper."

There was a pause, and the chorus response didn't come. Instead, a protest did.

"Aunty Augusta, who did not want Patto in her house?" Odion and Iyase chimed, almost simultaneously.

---

[3] 'So be it'.

## *TRAVEL TALES OF MY FATHER MR. JONES*

"My grandchildren, we never pay back evil with evil."

"Isee o."

Odion and Iyase suddenly started sobbing. Patto had been like a father to them, and they both understood that he would be gone for good.

"Odion and Iyase, you know that since we lost papa and mama, grandma has been all we have. Please continue to help grandma on the farm and don't leave her to do the work all alone. We pray that our gods will keep her strong and healthy so that we, too, will be able to give her some support in old age."

"I am already old, *jare*[4]. I just want to see you my grandchildren doing okay in life then I can depart in peace."

Four years flew by for Patto, and during his holidays, he spent it with Chief. It was his way of saying 'thank you' to Chief. Chief would usually use

---

[4] A Nigerian expression used to lay emphasis on a sentence.

## *PATTO*

him as his personal assistant to run errands here and there. Even though Augusta did not like the idea, she liked how serviceable Patto was. She knew that her own children could not be trusted like Patto, and soon, Patto became Chief's trusted ally, handling all Chief's personal transactions and withdrawing of huge sums of money from the bank for him. Chief loved Patto and wished that his own children would turn out like Patto.

Chief's children lived a wasteful life. They partied and spent money recklessly. They were irresponsible. They were not doing so well at school. Patto was producing excellent results and graduated in a record time while Chief's children had extra courses to complete at their various universities. There was an unspoken hatred and jealousy between Patto and Chief's children – Ronnie and Edna. They were civil with Patto, but deep down, they didn't like him, also because it was clear that their father preferred him.

Patto was happy to have a place to lay his head. After his graduation from the university, his search for a job began. His vision was to work in an Oil and Gas company or a top conglomerate, where he could build a career and advance in his studies. He had his younger siblings to look after. They also deserved a chance to go to the university. Any little money that Patto made was sent for the upkeep of his younger siblings and the maintenance of their grandma who was now frail. Age was catching up with her, and age-related ailments like arthritis were on standby.

It was commonly believed that Lagos was the land of opportunities; the commercial nerve centre of Nigeria. Patto put in job applications everywhere he knew, and nothing worked. Nigeria had a teeming population of about 170 million people. About 20 million youth were looking for job opportunities. Jobs came mainly through whom one knew.

Patto had made up his mind that if he couldn't secure a job, he would travel to America to attempt the American dream. He shared his dream with Chief, who concurred that it would be a brilliant idea.

Chief knew that if Patto travelled, he would achieve success, but Chief didn't want to feel like he had failed in the upbringing of his kids. When he mentioned the idea to Augusta, without hesitation,

### *PATTO*

Augusta suggested that Chief should send Ronnie to the US as well.

"That's not a good idea," Chief murmured.

"What's not good about the idea? Sending your nephew to America while your son is right here is a good idea, eh?"

"We both know that Ronnie is very irresponsible. Here, he is under our own noses, unable to manage himself. What will happen to him when he gets to a place where there is no support or guidance for him?"

"He will survive. Maybe that will make him sit up," Augusta declared.

Chief knew too well that he wasn't going to win the war with her, so he gave up and agreed to send Ronnie to the States. Ronnie did not have any game plan. He didn't have a clue what he would do when he got to the States. He was sent off nonetheless, with 20,000 USD as a start-off money to enable him to settle down.

Six months later, Patto left for the US with only 500 USD. Despite all the assistance Patto rendered to Chief, he was rewarded with a ticket to the States and Basic Travelling Allowance of 500 USD. It was one of

## *TRAVEL TALES OF MY FATHER MR. JONES*

the cruel realities of life and carefully orchestrated by Augusta. Patto, on the other hand, was grateful that he had been offered a ticket and helped with his visa processing. He knew he had determination and that he would make it. It was just a matter of time. As far as Augusta was concerned, it was a matter of 'my son must succeed' by crook or foul means. She couldn't stand seeing Chief bestow all his confidence on Patto. She knew too well that Patto was of immense service to the household whereas their own children could not be trusted as they lived irresponsible lives and squandered the wealth of their parents. Their children's education adventure was a mishap. They all graduated with third-class degrees after spending extra time at the university. Were it not for their father's wealth, there would have been no hope for them in life.

Ronnie got to the US and continued with his life of delusion. He got entangled with the wrong crowd and before long his life was in a mess. He was always ringing home and asking for money. His life in America was like another conduit for draining funds. Chief could barely cope with his incessant demands

## *PATTO*

for funds with the promise to sort it out once he got settled.

Patto did not have a soft landing like Ronnie. In fact, he had a very tough time when he first arrived in the States. He worked as a security guard at night and in the tills during the day. During weekends, he attended a local community college to improve himself. After spending three years in the US, Patto earned his first master's degree. After seven years, in the US, Patto naturalised as an American citizen. He had secured a good job in Texas and was working through his career and studying for his second master's. Ronnie, meanwhile, was running from pillar to post, being embattled with child support for his various 'baby mamas'. Chief was really getting fed up with him.

Patto invited Chief to visit him in Texas. Chief was heartbroken that a child who was not his, whom he sent off to the States with only 500 USD could, within a space of eight years, send him a ticket to visit him while his own blood was still requesting assistance from him. It was always a case of 'this last chance dad, everything is going to be okay', and Chief had been hearing that for about eight years with no end to the promises in sight.

While studying at the university, Patto had formed a strong friendship with a contemporary of his – Dennis. It was a union that stood the test of time. Dennis was coming to the US to visit Patto. While at the university, Patto had a habit of smoking weed. He smoked weed all through his stay at the university. Dennis always admonished Patto to quit the habit, and Patto would only remark with a smile and the phrase "Dennis, you would not understand why I smoke this weed. Someday, I will tell you my story."

It was on the balcony of Patto's home in Houston, Texas that he told the story. They had savoured a meal of grilled salmon, steamed vegetables, and grilled plantain. They were now washing it down with a glass of Spanish wine and having the evening air soak them.

"Dennis, you remember I had promised that one day, I will tell you my story?"

"Yes, you did."

"Well, after my parents passed away, my siblings and I were shoved from one relative to another, and all of them avoided us like a plague. They did not want to have anything to do with us, and we ended up in the village with our grandmother. I started smoking weed. The people I used to smoke weed with accepted me. They became *my new family*. I smoked weed all through my life in secondary school up to university when I met you, and you influenced me to stop smoking weed. I never told you, but I admired how you walked alone back at the university and how you were so focused. I told myself that if Dennis didn't really have friends and he was not smoking, I had no excuse for smoking weed. But I am aware that it was the association with the smokers that gave me a social life and made me pull through life. So to cut the long story short, it was this *ikpo* that saved me throughout my days as a youngster till I met with you and you introduced me to the higher power."

# 7: REMEMBER MARK

Weighing over one hundred and fifty kilogrammes, he could barely fit into the chair. The desk in the classroom could barely contain him. The desk had to press against his lap or he had to sit sideways in order to relax a little. Big Bondus was seventeen years old and had a large frame for his age. His head was massive like one of those giant watermelons in Walmart and his body was like a hippo's body. He walked in a slow manner and stood at six feet three inches tall. Big Bondus was repeating the year and was a little older than the other students in his class. He had extra-large palms and wore a US size 16 for footwear. His mates called him Big B.

## *REMEMBER MARK*

In his class, students teased and bullied him. The younger and slimmer kids would make a remark at him and run off. Some would try some physically unpleasant games with him and run away. They all knew that before he got off the chair, which was always a task for him, to dash after them, they would have long escaped to a safe zone. Big B had learnt to cope with this. He would often times ignore the kids and, once in a while, stretch his hands to see if he could grab any of them. Yet, they would be elusive. His greatest weapons were his large palms, big frame, and large feet. Once, he stamped on a boy's foot and almost crushed it.

Big B had reported to teachers too many times that the fingers could count, and in turn, the teachers had given out many warnings to erring students and meted out consequences to the bullies. It was a really tricky situation that needed a sustainable solution.

Big B was not exactly the bright type. The processing speed in his brain needed an upgrade. It took him a very long time to process simple instructions. He was a boy who had made genuine progress over the three years he spent repeating the grade. He had had about three English teachers and was used to being shoved about. Because of his weight and bulk, he wasn't very quick at doing things physically. For example, if everyone walked down to the grocery shop at an average speed of ten minutes per kilometre, he would trudge along at twenty minutes per kilometre.

Seated in the marking room, the English teachers had been marking for about one hour. Sometimes when a teacher stumbled across some hilarious item, he or she would share it with the rest of the team, and the team would either smile, laugh, or grimace. Somebody stumbled across an answer booklet that had the numbering on the exam paper neatly copied out onto the answer sheet. Then the candidate started copying down the questions one by one without any of the questions being answered. The marker passed the sheet to another teacher to have a look at in case there was something he was missing. The other teacher had a look at the script, and said, "There is nothing here, except the numbering." It meant that the student would score a zero.

"That must be one of my students," Mr. Itula said. "It must be Big B."

Since it was only identification numbers that the candidates wrote, it was difficult to tell whose script it was. In addition, teachers were not allowed to mark or see the scripts of their students. When the script was turned, it had the writing "Good to see you" at the back. Only one student could do that. It took him a full year to learn that sentence and the moment he learnt it, he sang it like a song. Anytime he saw anyone, it was always, "Good to see you."

Walking down the long hallway, Mr. Kurt saw a little crowd ahead of him and heard some noises. The noisy crowd was apparently laughing, jeering, or cheering at something. Scenes like those were not unpopular in school at lunchtime. An all-male school like St. Bartholomew's had boys with high levels of testosterone and what you would expect was anything that took some energy out of them would be welcomed. The students would either play football, basketball, or table tennis during the lunch break. Some would look for a quiet corner to just sit and have a chat with their mates. Unfortunately, some would stumble across trouble or seek to make some trouble or revenge on perceived foes. It was all adventure for them. It made the school tick.

As Mr. Kurt neared the crowd that was jeering and booing, he peeped inside the circle. Mark was being held by his two shoulders in mid-air by Big B.

Mark was one of those kids who thought he was smart. He was pesky. He loved picking on Big B. He would poke at him and run off. He would snatch his pen and dart away. He thought he was invincible. It was an unexpected meeting when he opened the big door to jet into the hallway and there was Big B right in front of him. It was too late to turn back. Big B's patience had paid off.

'Now, I got you, you little git and I am going to teach you a lesson, boy', Mr. Kurt could imagine Big B saying.

Mark was perspiring on the forehead. He had no strength left to resist. Nobody dared to go separate him from Big B. Big B might have been slow, but if he got a hold of anyone, the person was as good as dead meat. Mr. Kurt likened him to Lennie in the

## REMEMBER MARK

legendary tale of *Of Mice and Men*. Mr. Kurt parted his way through the crowd and walked towards the big man. By that time, Big B was shaking Mark with much vigour.

Mr. Kurt was scared for Mark. He tapped Big B on the shoulder, but Big B didn't turn around.

Mr. Kurt tapped him again and whispered in a stern voice, "Let go of him."

Big B turned around, looked at Mr. Kurt, and dropped Mark to the ground, but didn't let go. He instead pulled Mark towards himself and lounged his head at Mark's head. Mark was dazed. He was disoriented and swirling. Mr. Kurt had to approach the situation with caution because, once, a teacher was manhandled by an angry student because the teacher did not approach things with caution.

"Hello, big man. I am glad you have taught him a lesson," Mr. Kurt said.

Big B beamed with a smile. He must have thought, 'I am not in trouble after all'.

Mr. Kurt knew what would be working on his mind was, 'I might as well make him dead meat because I am already in trouble and I was caught red-handed'. But hearing those words calmed him down two notches.

For Mr. Kurt, it was a case of 'fifty percent damage was better than a hundred percent damage'.

"I think he has learnt his lesson, let go of him now," Mr. Kurt continued.

Big B pulled Mark one more time to himself and head-butted him the second time, then let go of him. Mark fell to the ground, motionless. Mr. Kurt removed Big B from the scene and called for support and an ambulance.

For the rest of the term, Big B lived in peace. Unofficially, the caution phrase for bullies in the school was: 'Remember Mark'.

*REMEMBER MARK*

***TRAVEL TALES OF MY FATHER MR. JONES***

## *8: THE DRUMS CALLED HIM*

In the round table where he sat in the large hall, laughter reigned, jokes were cracked and banter and pleasantries were exchanged. There was a constant stream of folks to this table to pay obeisance to one man. This man was full of smiles and cheer, regardless of his situation. He infected everybody with his robust cheerfulness. His friend, Sule, an old ally stayed by his left side and they conversed. His wife, Surita sat at his immediate right and some of his wife's friends sat on the other curved side of the table. Surita was decked in gold-coloured apparel – *Buba* and *Iro*[5]. She tied a purple headgear, in a local

---

[5] A type of traditional outfit in Yorubaland, Nigeria, worn by ladies.

style. It had taken about two hours for the headgear to be tied and her face to be made up. The make-up artist was booked one month in advance for the event. It was the celebration of the exit of Pa. Kunle Montegro, the last stock of the returnee slaves who came with the Liberty ship to Freetown. His great-great-great-grandfather was Mr. Montegro who schooled in the famous Fourah Bay College, Sierra Leone, and returned to Nigeria as an eminent historian scholar par excellence.

The man himself, Mr. Kunle Montegro, was simplicity personified. Though money was never a problem for the Kunles, they lived knowing the value of money. When it came to party times, the Kunles sure did know how to reconfigure themselves to make the moment count. Surita was the type who loved dancing. She would dance and dance till the musicians would run out of praise-singing for her. The culture in the Yoruba land of Nigeria was that when it was dance time during an event, the celebrants would go to the centre stage and dance. Family and friends of the celebrant would join them on the centre stage and dance along with them. It is during this epic moment that monies are sprayed. Different denominations of naira and other currencies are sprayed. The musicians would praise the sprayers because they also benefit from the flow of the largesse. Surita was bending and digging it in, as the crowd cheered. Beads of perspiration turned to rivulets. The drums talked non-stop.

Kunle bent his head over to Sule, and whispered, "I hear the drums calling me."

Sule laughed and playfully slapped Kunle on his back.

The drums talked on. The conga drums were handled by drummers who understood the drum. It awakened something in Kunle. Kunle nodded and oscillated his head to the right, and to the left, swung his shoulders, and began to sing along. The tune playing was 'Miracle Miracle'. It was a very popular tune, but what made the difference was that the talking drums were handled by the trio of Olawale, Adesina, and Akeem. The conga drum specialists were from drummer families. They had a history with

## *THE DRUMS CALLED HIM*

drums and a connection with drums as if drumming was encrypted in their DNA.

Looking over to the platform at the drummers reminded one of the synchronised movement during Olympics swimming. Their shoulders vibrated at the same time, their knees buckled at the same time, and their waists rolled at the same time. It was synchronised. Ayinde, the singer had moved from the song 'Miracle Miracle' to eulogising Surita, who was spraying wads of naira notes. Friends and family members followed suit in the spraying. The centre stage seemed like it was possessed. The spirit of the drumming had seized the drummers and they gave different renditions of waltzes and dances.

The audience chuckled. People laughed and lauded the dancers. Phones were videoing and taking photos. Photographers made brisk business. They took unauthorised photos of folks and quickly printed them off in different sizes of paper and sold the photos to the individuals. Some paid for the photos while some didn't. They just grabbed their copies. A woman was overheard shouting at a photographer, "Who asked you to take photos of me, eh?"

## *TRAVEL TALES OF MY FATHER MR. JONES*

People ate tons. The ones who ate the most were the uninvited guests. They called the food servers the most, ordering different items on the menu. They ordered drinks incessantly. Surita's name was announced over the loudspeakers.

*"The one who cannot see poor people and ignore them. The one who is as beautiful as a pearl. The one who is unparalleled in beauty. The one who is 60 and looks 16. The one who holds the title of sweet sixteen."*

The tempo of the drumming changed and the drummers were seized and warped in perspiration. Their hands received an extra surge of energy. They beat the drums harder. Ayinde stepped away from his microphone, and the atmosphere received an extra charge. The photographers were busy showing photos to Kunle. They had captured him in moments he hadn't realised. Kunle loved photos taken when he was not prepared. That was his weakness. He was inundated with choices. All of a sudden, he flung the photos to the floor, engaged the reverse gear of his motorised wheelchair, and rode out of the table.

"Where are you going?" Sule asked.

"The drums call me," he replied.

## *THE DRUMS CALLED HIM*

He rode in royalty to the floor. People parted ways for him, bringing to mind the scenario of the parting of the red sea. He rode straight to the centre stage. He undulated his right and left shoulders, moved his neck back and forth, and spun his wheelchair around. People cheered.

Surita moved over to her husband. "Honey, are you okay?"

"Do I not seem okay?"

The drummers were in a frenzy now.

Ayinde switched his eulogies to Kunle.

*"The one that even the chair could not stop. The one who hails from the city of the big rock. The one whose bravery and acclaim are known far and wide. The one whom the gods even recognise as the wise one. The one who recognises that the drummers are from the ancestral lineage."*

The drums switched the notes. Ayinde stopped eulogising. The drums were now talking. Kunle took his right hand and grabbed his dead right leg. Took his left hand and gave extra support to his right leg. He propped his right leg on the floor.

"Honey, what are you doing? You are going to hurt yourself."

## *TRAVEL TALES OF MY FATHER MR. JONES*

He did the same thing to his left leg.

Sule bent over his friend, and asked, "What are you doing, Kunle?"

"What does it seem like I am doing?" Kunle replied.

With all his strength, Kunle grabbed Sule's neck and clung to it, almost toppling Sule over. He propped himself up and buckled. Everybody rushed to support him. He shooed them away from himself. He used his two hands and clasped Sule, as if in a tight wrestle, then he steadied himself and began to stabilise. A new surge of energy flowed to his legs. He let go of the clasp. He swayed a little. The crowd rushed to support him again.

"Stop!" he yelled.

Ayinde grabbed the microphone.

*"My father told me how good a dancer you were. You could do the acrobat. You could do the somersault. You, the fearless one that even the non-functionality of your leg could not stop. The one who danced and won laurels. Welcome home!"*

The drummers changed the beat; it became authentic. The drums spoke in a language Kunle alone understood.

### *THE DRUMS CALLED HIM*

"The drums call me. I hear them loud and clear," Kunle said to himself.

He put one leg forward, then another, and yet another.

The hall was agog now. He swirled around, grabbed Surita, and began the talking drum dance.

**TRAVEL TALES OF MY FATHER MR. JONES**

# 9: THE FIGHT: FROM THE DIARY OF MR. AKPAN, ANOTHER TEACHER AT SHC

I dialled the emergency number, and we waited for the ambulance and the police. Everybody wanted to know how I did what I did to Marcus B, the notorious. My fame spread like wildfire across the whole school and neighbouring schools.

'Mark *tiptoed* into the room and *slipped* into the bed. The duvet *stank* of damp. The room needed airing, but how could he do that with temperatures plummeting to minus sixteen degrees Celsius? The heating was only turned on in very desperate hours.

### *THE FIGHT: FROM THE DIARY OF MR. AKPAN, ANOTHER TEACHER AT SHC*

He was tired of *loading himself* with garments as if he was a washing machine.'

"We are going to examine the effect that these verbs create in the sentences in the passage above. What effect does the verb *tiptoed* create, Dellon?"

"It creates the effect of stealing," Dellon answered.

The class roared into a fit of laughter.

"Why stealing?" I asked.

"Why would he tiptoe into his own bed? Couldn't he walk into his room?" Dellon carried on.

"Maybe he does not want to wake up people in his house," Angode shouted.

"No, the text does not say that there were other people in the room or house," Nick chipped in.

"But the question Mr. Akpan asked was what effect does tiptoe create?" Dellon said. "And to me, it creates the effect of stealing, because he does not want to be noticed or seen coming in, and that is what thieves or burglars do."

"Very good answer, Dellon."

## *TRAVEL TALES OF MY FATHER MR. JONES*

The classroom door flew open. "Mr. Akpan, Mr. Akpan, please come right now. Come right now. Ms. J needs you. There is a big fight out in Ms. J's classroom."

Two thoughts quickly went through my head. 'How can I leave twenty-three students unattended? What if something went wrong?'

Another thought was 'Maybe the students in Ms. J's class were in serious danger and needed help. Ms. J was a lady and probably couldn't contain the situation."

I had to take a chance there, and I went for it.

Quickly, I sent the class captain to Ms. Pickjo's office with a note for help while I darted out to the corridor. Out in the corridor, Muwanga was on top of Mallete. Mallette's back was pinned to the floor. Muwanga was thumping Mallette so hard, left, right, left, right, and Mallette was struggling to breathe.

I raised my voice, and shouted, "Stand back everybody and give way."

Ms. J couldn't have dealt with that. I had never seen such a fight in the past eight years I had been in

## *THE FIGHT: FROM THE DIARY OF MR. AKPAN, ANOTHER TEACHER AT SHC*

the school. Mallete toppled Muwanga and was struggling to get on top of him, but Muwanga was holding on tightly to his throat. With all my strength I lurched straight at Muwanga's hand and unclipped them from Mallete's throat. They both sprang up and looked like two cockerels about to relaunch an attack. I darted in between the two of them to separate them, and a punch landed on my belly.

"Aaaargh!" I tightened my belly muscles, and said, "Muwanga, keep your hands and feet to yourself."

"Fuck off, Mr. Akpan. I am gonna teach that idiot a lesson. You don't fuck with me," he ranted.

Instinctively, I outstretched my arms around Muwanga's body and clasped his body and arms. That incapacitated him, as his main weapons were securely fastened by my clasp. I then jacked him away. He struggled by attempting to kick and wriggle himself free but my clasp was just too tight. The students were cheering, "Bang him! Bang him!"

By that time, Mr. Edwards, the senior teacher on duty, had arrived and had rushed Mallete into Ms. J's room and locked the door. I heard a constant banging on the door. It was Mallette wanting to escape. Muwanga was struggling to escape out of my grip to launch another offensive at Mallette. I managed to take him down the stairs to the head teacher's office. He was dangling in my grip. He just needed to be evacuated from that scene.

I had always been of the opinion that there should be a permanent guy on duty in such a school like that, who could be called in to end fights. The women could not handle those types of fight. Being a body builder-cum-martial artist, I was struggling to drag the guy into the office. He tried to use his legs to tighten and curl on the railings just to slow our onward proceeding down the stairs. As I came down the stairs and was about to make my way into the office area, with Muwanga still struggling with me to let go, Marilyn the new arts teacher, saw me, and started, "Sir, can you let go of him? You cannot hold a student like this."

I ignored her, as Muwanga kept shouting, "Mr. Akpan, let go of me. Mr. Akpan, let go of me."

I replied, "No, I am not letting go of you until you calm down, and you are safe in the office."

## *THE FIGHT: FROM THE DIARY OF MR. AKPAN, ANOTHER TEACHER AT SHC*

Marilyn went on, "Sir, let go of him. Sir, let go of him."

I thought 'Damn!'

By that time, Ms. Eastmond, the office secretary, who was walking by saw the pandemonium and joined Marilyn in condemning my action and requesting I let go of Muwanga.

"Can you girls open the office door please and stop asking me to let go of Muwanga?"

They said "No", unless I let go of Muwanga.

My first instinct was to kick them out of my way, but I thought, 'Be calm and don't let go of this guy. Get him safely in the office and then deal with issues later.

Ms. J had come down by that time and helped to open the office door to get Muwanga in.

My shirt was spotted with blood stains and all ruffled up. My watch was not on my wrist, and my tie was mangled up.

"Akpan, thanks ever so much; thanks so much. Over my twenty-two years of experience as a teacher, I have never seen such a fight," Ms. J managed to utter. "I have your watch. The strap is cut."

"No worries," I said.

Inside Marilyn's office, Marilyn went on about how disappointed she was with me and how she should have called the police for me for manhandling a pupil.

I sat still and listened to her. I was calm and quiet. I thought within me 'An overzealous Newly Qualified Teacher'. 'Get your facts first; get your facts first before you judge', rang through my mind.

"Listen, Marilyn, I really owe you no apology. You might as well have called the police. I came here to give you a piece of advice. I have been teaching for eight years and I know about fights and handling and manhandling pupils, okay? Now Muwanga and Mallete were involved in the deadliest fight I have ever seen in my teaching career. In case you did not know, please know today that you can physically restrain a pupil if he is in danger to himself or others around him. You have to get him to a safe place first, and that was what I had to do."

I took time to explain to her the background of the fight and how I was trying to get Muwanga to the

## *THE FIGHT: FROM THE DIARY OF MR. AKPAN, ANOTHER TEACHER AT SHC*

office. I expressed my disappointment at the way she handled the whole issue. She had not been supportive and did not offer any help, instead, she gave very uncomplimentary remarks in front of other students. Those students were going to take those vibes home to their parents, probably saying, "Oh guess what mum or guess what dad? A teacher in our school, Mr. Akpan, was manhandling a student, and Ms. Marilyn was asking him to let go of the student and he wouldn't let go."

"Is that what you want? Is that what you want the parents to hear? How good you are and how you love the students?" I asked. "And how bad I am and how I manhandle the students? Is that what you want? Huh? Well, I don't care what you said and the damage you have caused. I did the right thing, and if I were to do it again, I would do it exactly the same way. But next time, before you speak in a situation like that, let it be with guarded lips because you cannot undo this damage you have caused."

When I looked into her eyes, I saw silent tears streaming down her face.

## *TRAVEL TALES OF MY FATHER MR. JONES*

"Mr. Akpan, I am so sorry for what I said and did. I never realised that the fight was that serious and that you were actually in the process of diffusing a very serious conflict. I am so, so sorry."

"Well, sorry does not undo all the damage you have caused now by your careless talk, can it?"

"I know it can't, but please, is there any space in your heart to forgive me?"

"It's okay. I have forgiven you." I replied. "I gotta go now."

"To show that you have truly forgiven me, please give me a hug."

"Trust me, I have forgiven you. I don't need to give you a hug to prove that."

*THE FIGHT: FROM THE DIARY OF MR. AKPAN, ANOTHER TEACHER AT SHC*

## 10: THE TUNNEL

As the Navegante boat slipped out of the harbour making her way into the huge water, I took a moment to familiarise myself with my environment. I took a walk around the lower deck and finally eased myself into my seat. Sitting opposite me was a man with rough hair and untrimmed beards. He wore a baseball cap with the inscription 'Survivor'. His T-shirt had the same inscription. I was a little intrigued. He rested his chin on his palm as he stared into the water. Then I noticed that his tanned arm had the same inscription.

The wind was high and it was a little noisy.

"Hello," I said.

"Hello," he responded.

## *THE TUNNEL*

"Mr Survivor, is that your name?" I hollered pointing at his fez, T-shirt, and arm.

"Yes. I am a survivor, and it is my name," he replied with what looked like a grin.

"Oh wow. First time I am seeing someone with their name inscribed on their arm."

"Yups," he muttered, then added, "There is always a first time."

With hands outstretched, we shook hands.

"Call me Uwem."

"Darnell Survivor."

What was supposed to be a three-hour trip in the Pacific Ocean spotting whales and dolphins turned out to be a harvest of tales and an unforgettable encounter with a survivor of one of the most horrible quarry accidents in Chile. Listening to Darnell narrate this blood chilling experience of how he and two of his mates braced and raced against all the horrors of the abandoned tunnel, they had managed to access in the underground labyrinth in the battle for survival.

Down the deep tunnel, he walked on. He was tired. He was exhausted. He sat and leaned his back to the wall of the tunnel. He didn't know how much longer he had to trudge that dark path. There wasn't a sign of an end in sight. A big rodent tried to bite his feet, but he was protected by his weather-beaten safety shoes. The stench was a part and parcel of him now. He had mastered the art of surviving the stench – no moaning or whining, just keep trudging on. He had lost two friends, Jugger and Ecklewood. Could he be the one who would perhaps make it to the end? The world would need to hear their escape story.

Jugger had had an infection and needed antibiotics badly. The sanitation was poor. They answered their nature's call in the tunnel. How worse could things get? They were drinking water from the same tunnel. They would just mutter some incantations over the drink and scoop it with their bare hands, and down it went through their oesophagus. They were the very hands that did the job of toilet paper, paved the path in the tunnel, scooped water, and were the pallbearer of the water that sent Jugger home. Nothing made sense anymore. The key word was survival.

For eight days they had been trudging that god-forsaken tunnel. How much longer would they

## *THE TUNNEL*

remain in there? They watched the ghost leave Jugger. They held him, embraced him, and told him to hold on.

"I can't," he kept saying.

"Jugger, just hold on," Ecklewood said.

"For how long?" Jugger asked.

"For as long as it takes us to get to the end of the tunnel," Darnell said.

Jugger let out a loud grunt. The pain was excruciating. They all held him. He was panting for breath. He gasped and coughed, and spat out the specimen on the tunnel wall. It was too dark to see the colour. It smelt like blood and infected phlegm. He coughed some more. He was choking. And then in a split second, the atmosphere around them changed. It became a little mysterious and unbearably quiet like a stranger had just arrived. A little uninvited guest had made an entry into their sorrow.

"Are you ready?" he whispered to Jugger.

"Yes, I am. I have been waiting for you. Why did it take you so long to come?"

"The chord of the alliance took a bit longer to break."

## *TRAVEL TALES OF MY FATHER MR. JONES*

"I am ready. Let's go."

Jugger was gone. No time to grieve, no time to cry. It was time to move on. What would they do with his corpse? Would they drag it along for the rest of the journey? They took turns clutching his body. They cried. They left him behind and moved on.

"What a way to abandon a friend in death," Ecklewood managed to say, as they plodded on.

They were both lost in their own world. The stark reality that stared them in the face was that what had happened to Jugger could have happened to any of them. Was that how they would have ended up? Dead in the tunnel of death? Abandoned in the tunnel of death to rot away. Knowing that their carcass would be meat for the rodents that lived in the tunnel was just too sad. Perhaps it might have been better to be meat for lions than rodents. It seemed and sounded a bit more dignified than meat for rodents, pests, and bugs.

Ecklewood buckled under the weight of those thoughts. He slumped to the floor and wept like a baby. He was inconsolable.

## *THE TUNNEL*

"Let's go back and get Jugger," he managed to say in between sobs.

"No, we can't go back," Darnell declared. "We can't. Forward ever, backward never."

A fat rodent scurried past. Bats squeaked, and different sounds were heard. Bugs and insects that felt their privacies were being intruded, reacted, and resisted.

"Listen, buddy, this is tough on both of us, but we got to move on. We can't afford to waste energy. We need every reservoir of strength in us to push on," Darnell said.

"I know, I know, but we can't leave him to be food to these pests. He was a brave man. He should have a proper burial and not be left here to be food for bugs and pests" Ecklewood carried on.

"But if we had put him in a casket and lowered him to the grave, he would still be food to earthworms and bugs, and stuff," Darnell countered.

"At least, he would have a proper burial, where we can always go back and visit and that's more dignifying."

## *TRAVEL TALES OF MY FATHER MR. JONES*

Three days later, Ecklewood announced that he couldn't push forward anymore. They had been eleven days in the tunnel without food, clean water, and sanitation.

It was a quick move, Ecklewood got it by the tail, pulled it to itself, and squeezed the neck, and within secs, it was dead. He brought out the lighter from his pocket and roasted the rodent. In three minutes a meal was ready. Darnell couldn't stand the sight. He became sick. Some slimy yellowish stuff came out from his belly. Ecklewood munched at the poor creature, squashing every bone as he cracked on.

Ten minutes later, Ecklewood became very sick. His temperature shot up. Darnell placed the back of his hand on his forehead, and the temperature could almost boil an egg. Two hours later, Ecklewood passed away peacefully.

"If you ever make it to where there is light, tell Rosalind that in the attic, there is a chest, and in its bottom compartment, there is an exercise book. All the details she needs to know are in there," were his last words.

## *THE TUNNEL*

Darnell was devastated. He wept himself to sleep. He dreamed that he saw light. He dreamed that he saw faces again, that he ate real food, and that he was sleeping in a bed. He dreamed that he heard voices and people singing. He dreamed that he was back in a real house. He awoke to the cold stiffness of Ecklewood's body. He lifted Ecklewood's head off him and grabbed the cold body. He moved on. It was like a new surge of energy came to him. A new charge of electrostatics enveloped him, and in the strength of that energy, he moved on. He walked and crawled and crouched till he felt that perhaps the time was near for him to go the way of his mates.

He started hearing what seemed like voices. He inched forward, then he bumped into something. He felt it. It was a ladder. He stepped on it and clung to it. He muscled all his strength and took the first step. He was drained. There was no energy in him. He took the next climb. He almost fell over. His foot slipped and he buckled. He held on to what seemed like life. 'Could this be the end?' he wondered. If he had made it this far, would the last lap fail him? He panted. He took a rest. Then with all the will within him, he pulled himself up and surged forward till he bumped into a metal. He knocked at it. He banged his head hard at it.

"I can't give up now", he mumbled, then repeated, "I can't give up now."

The light struck his eyes almost blinding him. He passed out.

He awoke several hours later in a hospital. He was alive and had made it through the tunnel of death.

Three months later, he was speaking to an audience about how he made it through that dark tunnel.

"What kept you through those dark hours, Mr. Darnell?"

"Hope. Just hope! I had only one thing left. Faith. I just hoped that by any streak of chance, I would make it. Jugger and Ecklewood were the finest men I ever worked with in my life, stronger people, yet they did not make it."

## *THE TUNNEL*

## *A WORD FROM THE AUTHOR*

I seek to bring the art of storytelling alive once more from a written perspective. My culture and roots are etched in the great art of storytelling. Great lessons of life are provided from storytelling sessions. Education, art, history, geography, science, anthropology, social studies, medicine, and religion can all be traced back to this ancient art. In traditional African societies and other ancient traditions, this was a great skill that was revered. In kings' palaces and communities, skilled storytellers served as resident literary artists, poets, and/or minstrels. It is through this art that knowledge has been transmitted from generation to generation. Through this art, I seek to reconnect my audience with the experience of learning and enriching the readers' minds, whilst enjoying the art of narration.

This collection **_Travel Tales of My Father Mr Jones_** is a continuation of the author's compilation of his life as a teacher and an expatriate living across different cities in the world.

If you wish to keep in touch with me or give me feedback on my book, please use any of the links below. I'll be happy to hear from you:

Email: uwemmbotumana@gmail.com

Instagram: @enrichyourmind.co.uk

Facebook: @enrichyourmind.stories.9

Twitter: @CostaBlue3

Tiktok: @uwemumana_enrichyourmind

Other books by the author are:

*Drums and Blues* (A collection of poems)

*Awakening The Troubadors* (An anthology of poems),

*Dead and Other Stories* – Volume 1 (A collection of short stories)

*Son Of The Soil and Other Stories* – Volume 2 (A

collection of short stories).

*I Can't Lie to Myself and Other Stories* – Volume 3 (A collection of short stories)